Baby cows are called calves and they drink milk. When they are about six months old, they start to eat grass.

Baby ducks are called ducklings. They have webbed feet.

A duckling's food is slugs.

JUNGLE ANIMALS

Many animals live in jungles and rainforests where it is hot and damp.

Baby tigers are called cubs.

cubs start hunting when they are about one year old.

Baby snakes are called hatchlings.

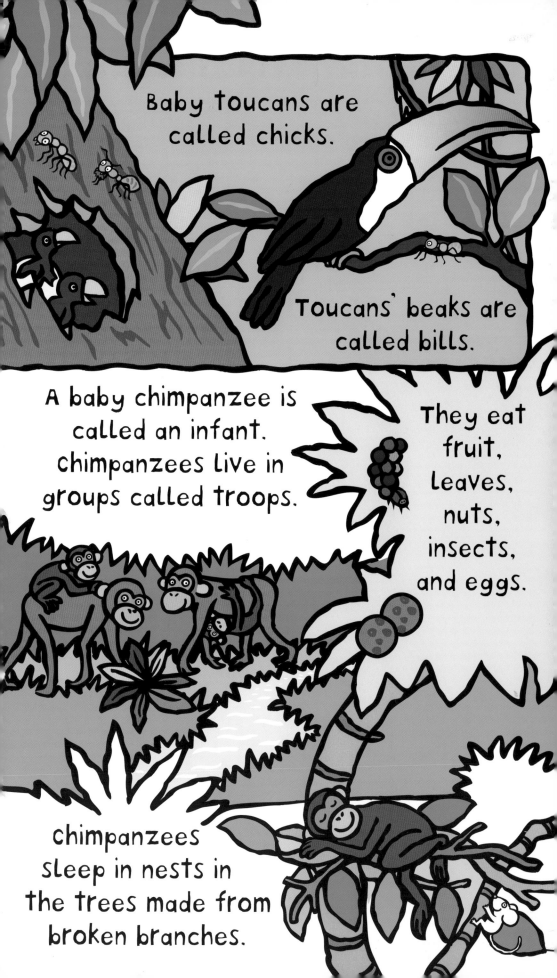

Baby toucans are called chicks.

Toucans' beaks are called bills.

A baby chimpanzee is called an infant. chimpanzees live in groups called troops.

They eat fruit, leaves, nuts, insects, and eggs.

chimpanzees sleep in nests in the trees made from broken branches.

BUSH ANIMALS

The outback of Australia
is very hot and dry.

Kookaburra
babies are
called chicks.
They feed on
worms and
small insects.

Baby kangaroos are called joeys.
They live on milk in their
mothers' pouches.

Baby koalas are called joeys, too. Their favorite food is eucalyptus leaves.

Platypus babies are called pups.

The platypus digs burrows in the riverbank using its webbed and clawed feet.

OCEAN ANIMALS

The ocean is home to some of the
biggest creatures in the world.

Baby dolphins are called calves.
They live in groups called pods.

Baby seahorses are
called fry.

They must
rise to the
surface as
soon as they
are born to
breathe.

Baby sharks are called pups.

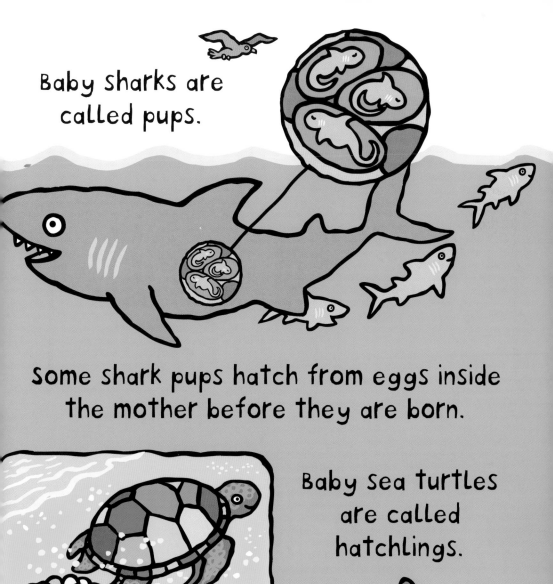

Some shark pups hatch from eggs inside the mother before they are born.

Baby sea turtles are called hatchlings.

Sea turtles lay eggs in the sand, then cover them up to keep them moist and safe.

POLAR ANIMALS

Some animals live in very cold places
like the Arctic and Antarctic.

Baby penguins are
called chicks.
Penguins cannot fly.

Baby whales are called calves.
Whales sometimes slide out of the water
onto the ice to try to catch
the penguins.